The Hidden World of

Hacke

Expressions

Elise Wallace

Contributing Author

Alison S. Marzocchi, Ph.D.

Consultant

Colleen Pollitt, M.A.Ed.
Math Support Teacher
Howard County Public Schools

Publishing Credits

Rachelle Cracchiolo, M.S.Ed., *Publisher*
Conni Medina, M.A.Ed., *Editor in Chief*
Dona Herweck Rice, *Series Developer*
Emily R. Smith, M.A.Ed., *Series Developer*
Diana Kenney, M.A.Ed., NBCT, *Content Director*
Stacy Monsman, M.A., *Editor*
Michelle Jovin, M.A., *Associate Editor*
Fabiola Sepulveda, *Graphic Designer*

Image Credits: p. 6 (bottom right) Maksym Kozlenko / Wikimedia Commons; p.6 (bottom left) 1971markus / Wikimedia Commons; p.7 Sal Veder / Associated Press; p.8 Courtesy Kevin Mitnick / Tolga Kates / Mitnick Security; p.9 AP Photo / Michael J. Okoniewski; p.10 Kristy Wigglesworth / Associated Press; p.12 Mikhail Japaridze / TASS / Getty Images; p.13 Kyodo/Newscom; p.14 REUTERS/Newscom; p.17 (top) Etienne De Malglaive / Getty Images; p.17 (bottom) Karimphoto / iStock; p.18 FABRICE COFFRINI/AFP/Getty Images; p.19 (top) U.S. Air Force; p.19 (bottom) Wolterk / iStock; p.22 Courtesy Ronald Rivest / MIT; p.24 (top) Volker Steger/Science Source; p.24 (bottom) Richard Kail / Science Source; p.25 Andy Aaron / IBM; p.26 Charles Kip Patterson/ZUMA Press/Newscom; p.27 Gene Blevins/ Polaris/Newscom; pp.28–29 DefCon / WikiVisually; all other images from iStock and/or Shutterstock.

Library of Congress Cataloging-in-Publication Data

Names: Wallace, Elise, author.
Title: The hidden world of hackers : expressions / Elise Wallace.
Description: Huntington Beach, CA : Teacher Created Materials, [2019] |
  Includes index. | Audience: Grades 4 to 6. |
Identifiers: LCCN 2018047791 (print) | LCCN 2018048605 (ebook) | ISBN
  9781425855291 (eBook) | ISBN 9781425858858 (pbk.)
Subjects: LCSH: Penetration testing (Computer security)--Juvenile literature.
  | Hacking--Juvenile literature. | Computer networks--Security
  measures--Juvenile literature.
Classification: LCC TK5105.59 (ebook) | LCC TK5105.59 .W345 2019 (print) |
  DDC 005.8/7--dc23
LC record available at https://lccn.loc.gov/2018047791

Teacher Created Materials
5301 Oceanus Drive
Huntington Beach, CA 92649-1030
www.tcmpub.com

ISBN 978-1-4258-5885-8
© 2019 Teacher Created Materials, Inc.
Printed in Malaysia
Thumbprints.21254

Table of Contents

The Who, What, and Why

Who are hackers? People often think of hackers as undercover agents who work alone and in secret. But that's not always the case. Many hackers work in networks, collaborating to achieve their goals. Hackers are computer-programming experts who use complex problem-solving to gain **access** to secure networks.

So, what exactly does it mean to *hack*? It's not a simple question. The word can mean many different things. For example, you can hack a tree by cutting it with great force. Or, you can have a hacking cough when you are sick. But the hacking that interests us refers to getting access, either legally or illegally, to information stored on computers.

The reason for hacking changes from person to person. Some hackers are compelled by curiosity. They want to know how a computer system works. Others are motivated by money. They use their abilities to steal information **anonymously**. But there are also hackers who do good! They make programs and networks more secure. These hackers find flaws in the designs of computer systems and fix them before they can cause problems.

A group of students learns about how a computer system works.

Hacker History

Hacking isn't a recent development. Modern hackers are part of a long and **storied** culture. Some of the first hackers became active in the 1960s and '70s. They **honed** their skills by breaking into phone networks, not computer systems.

These early hackers had a strange secret weapon—toy whistles! In 1955, the first hackers used the Davy Crockett Cat and the Canary Bird Call Flute toy whistles. In the mid 1960s, hackers used the whistles that came in Cap'n Crunch® cereal boxes to control phone systems. Among these hackers was Steve Wozniak, who would later become a cofounder of Apple®.

So, how were they able to hack telephones? They used the whistles to **mimic** the tones used by phones. By copying these tones, hackers were able to make long-distance phone calls for free. This system no longer works, though. Telephone companies have long since wised up to such tricks.

The hacking community grew in the 1980s and '90s. There were magazines for hackers that were written by hackers themselves. Online, programmers joined hacker groups. Each group had a different idea of what the purpose of hacking should be.

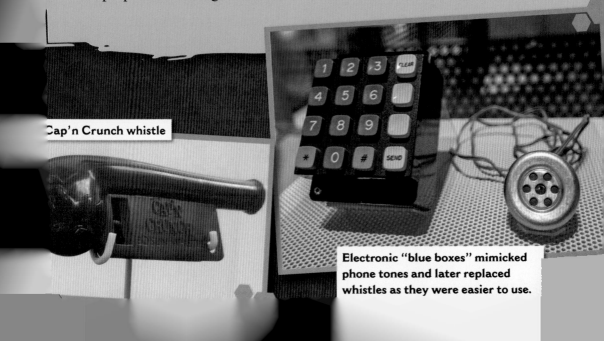

Cap'n Crunch whistle

Electronic "blue boxes" mimicked phone tones and later replaced whistles as they were easier to use.

Wozniak (right) unve[ils the]
Apple IIc computer w[ith Steve]
Jobs (left) and John S[culley,]
Apple president, in 1[984.]

LET'S EXPLORE MATH

Several years after 1960, hackers started hacking computers instead of phone networks. Choose all the expressions that represent "y years after 1960."

1960 ⟵————————————————⟶

y

A. $y + 1960$

B. $1960y$

C. $1960 - y$

D. $1960 + y$

The 1980s were an important time for hacker culture. Some of the most famous hackers emerged during this decade. Robert Tappan Morris was one of them. In 1988, he made a program that was meant to be harmless. The computer program was called a *worm*. Morris thought the worm would travel from computer to computer and hide. He wanted to see if it could be done. But Morris's worm actually ruined thousands of systems. He was fined $10,000. Morris also had to perform hundreds of hours of public service.

Though Morris faced criminal charges, he never lost interest in programming. Years later, he devoted his time to teaching. Morris teaches at the Massachusetts Institute of Technology (MIT). It is one of the most **esteemed** schools in the United States.

Another famous hacker of the 1980s was Kevin Mitnick. He was able to hack into government agencies as a teenager. At one point, Mitnick was on the FBI's most wanted list! He ended up serving time in prison. Once he was released, Mitnick put his hacker talents to better use. Today, he helps people improve their **cybersecurity**.

Kevin Mitnick

Morris walks out of the courthouse during his criminal trial.

Hacking in the 21st Century

Lately, the news has been ruled by hacking stories. Hackers have attacked some of the biggest companies in the world. In 2014, Sony® was hacked. A huge amount of the company's data was leaked. Private emails were made public. Whole systems were destroyed.

Hackers have made headlines around the world. In 2016, Russian hackers are **alleged** to have interfered with the American presidential election. Russian hackers allegedly made fake social media accounts and used them to target Americans. The aim of these hackers was to divide the American people.

But now that people are aware of such hackers, we can work hard to expose them. There are clues you can use to identify hackers. If a social media account posts many hateful items per day, be wary. Research the person behind the account. See whether their profile picture is real or just a **stock photo.**

These British newspapers report on phone hacking in 2011.

Imagine that a fake news story is rapidly spreading online. The number of times it was posted is shown by the expression 3^m. The m represents the number of minutes since the story was first posted.

1. How many times was the story posted after 5 minutes?

2. How many times was the story posted after 10 minutes?

3. Is the number of posts after 10 minutes double the number of posts after 5 minutes? Why or why not?

4. How many times was the story posted at minute 0? What does this mean?

Black Hats and White Hats

In the world of hacking, there are people who work to maintain security. There are others who work to destroy it. Those who hack illegally are called black hat hackers. They break into forbidden networks. Early in their careers, Mitnick and Morris were black hats. The hackers behind the Sony attacks and the Russian hackers with fake social media accounts are also examples of black hat hacking.

In contrast, there are people who work to improve cybersecurity. In other words, they protect digital files. These hackers are known as white hat hackers. They protect people from the damaging work performed by black hat hackers. White hats use their skills to find flaws in computer systems. They work hard to find all possible threats.

White hats are also called **ethical hackers**. Many companies need such hackers to protect their systems. If you are a computer-programming expert, there are many opportunities to work as a white hat hacker.

The leader of hacking group Humpty Dumpty— Vladimir Anikeyev—is put on trial in Moscow, Russia.

White hat teams compete in a cybersecurity contest.

LET'S EXPLORE MATH

Martina works as a computer programmer. She notices that the amount of time she spends on a project depends on the number of bugs, or errors, in the program. To plan her schedule, she must estimate how many minutes a project will take. To do this, she uses the expression $30 + 20 \times b^2$, where b represents the number of bugs.

1. What are Martina's estimates for finishing each project?
   a. Project A: 0 bugs
   b. Project B: 1 bug
   c. Project C: 5 bugs
   d. Project D: 10 bugs

2. Can she use the expression $30 + (20 \times b)^2$ to make the same estimates? Explain your reasoning.

White hat hackers use a number of methods in their work. Some of these methods are the same ones used by black hat hackers. To be effective, white hats must be able to think like criminals.

One tactic white hats use is called reverse engineering. To protect a system, a white hat needs to know how a system works and how it can be destroyed. Reverse engineering means to take a system apart. White hats protect systems by predicting how they may be broken down.

White hat hackers reverse engineer voting machine computers to search for evidence of black hat hackers.

Some hackers use virtual reality helmets to access people's data.

Another method is called social engineering. Black hats use this method to pose as other people. They pretend to be someone else—someone with access to private data. For example, a black hat may pose as someone from a credit card company to obtain the last four digits of a person's credit card. The hacker can use this information to control some of the person's accounts. After doing so, the black hat gains more data and takes over more accounts. Little by little, they trick others into helping hack into a person's life. White hat hackers use social engineering to outwit black hat hackers.

A Gray Area

White hat hackers must be well versed in the same software programs used by black hat hackers. This includes **malware** in all forms. One form of malware is called a *rootkit*. Black hats can hide rootkits on computers, and once hidden, rootkits can hide other software. White hats must be able to locate such malware to effectively protect people.

In addition to black hat and white hat hackers, there are also gray hat hackers. These people fall in the middle of black hats and white hats. Gray hat hackers don't harm others or do things to get ahead personally. But they dabble in areas that may seem wrong or illegal.

All three types of hackers can be **hacktivists**. Many hacktivists believe that information should be free and readily available. In 2011, the Egyptian government was oppressing many of its citizens. The country's internet access was shut down. Egyptian citizens were cut off from the world. Hacktivists used their skills to provide internet to Egyptians. Though their cause was noble, it was an illegal effort. This is why some hacking is hard to label as only bad or only good.

The hacktivist group who provided internet to Egyptians—Anonymous—is known for wearing these Guy Fawkes masks.

Egyptian citizens access the internet after Anonymous restored it.

People protest in Tahrir Square in Cairo, Egypt.

In the past, *hacker* has been a bad word. But that is changing with white hat hackers. More and more people are learning about the good work done by ethical hackers. Even the U.S. government sees the worth of training hackers. The U.S. Army has a cyber department. It is called the U.S. Army Cyber Command. The U.S. Navy, Air Force, and Marines also have teams trained in cybersecurity.

If a career in white hat hacking sounds interesting, there are many ways to work as an ethical hacker. Some people choose to get a degree in computer science. Others enroll in training programs on ethical hacking. A good place to start is by earning the Certified Ethical Hacker certification.

Ethical hackers are not always called white hats. They go by many names. In job postings, a white hat hacker might be called an intrusion analyst. Or they might be described as a cybersecurity threat analyst. But no matter their title, all ethical hackers need to be computer-programming experts!

People compete in an ethical hacking contest.

These U.S. Air Force members work in the cyber department.

The global security company Intel hires many ethical hackers.

19

Cybersecurity

So, what does the future have in store? Will hackers rule the world? After all, black hats keep getting better at hacking. That is why it is key that white hats keep finding new ways to protect data. Cybersecurity needs to evolve. Even though no one can see it, there is a high-tech race between black hat hackers and those who protect data.

To know where cybersecurity is going, first look at how computers process data. Almost all computers use a **binary system** to process information. This is a system that stores data using only zeros and ones. That means the images you see on screens, even the music you listen to, are read by computers as zeros and ones.

Computers that use a binary system are called classical computers. These are the machines we use at home and at school. There are tried-and-true methods of protecting data on these computers, including forms of **encryption**.

This key shows how to convert characters into binary code. Try coding your name.

Letter	Binary Code	Letter	Binary Code	Letter	Binary Code
A	01000001	S	01010011	k	01101011
B	01000010	T	01010100	l	01101100
C	01000011	U	01010101	m	01101101
D	01000100	V	01010110	n	01101110
E	01000101	W	01010111	o	01101111
F	01000110	X	01011000	p	01110000
G	1000111	Y	01011001	q	01110001
H	1001000	Z	01011010	r	01110010
I	1001001	a	01100001	s	01110011
J	1001010	b	01100010	t	01110100
K	1001011	c	01100011	u	01110101
L	1001100	d	01100100	v	01110110
M	1001101	e	01100101	w	01110111
N	1001110	f	01100110	x	01111000
O	1001111	g	01100111	y	01111001
P	1010000	h	01101000	z	01111010
Q	1010001	i	01101001		
R	01010010	j	01101010		

One common form of data encryption is called RSA. The RSA code is named after the three men who designed it—Ronald L. Rivest, Adi Shamir (AH-dee shuh-MEER), and Leonard M. Adleman. The **RSA algorithm** uses two large prime numbers per encryption. Each of these prime numbers can have hundreds of digits. The two primes are multiplied, and their product becomes part of the code. To crack the code, a hacker would have to determine which two prime numbers were used.

From a hacker's point of view, finding these two prime numbers is nearly impossible. A classical computer can work for decades and never find the primes that were used. It takes computers a long time to crack such codes because of the way they process data. The smallest form of information in classical computing is called a *bit*. A bit of data can only store a zero or a one. This creates limitations for computers. That is why it takes hackers so long to crack codes like the RSA algorithm.

Shamir, Rivest, and Adleman

The time it takes for computer programs to run depends on the size of the data set. Imagine that the expressions show how much time it takes for different programs to run. The d represents the number of data entries. Match each numerical expression to its verbal description.

1. $8 + d^2$
2. $(8 + d)^2$
3. $8 + 2d$
4. $8 \times d^2$

A. The running time is 8 minutes plus two minutes per data entry.

B. The running time is 8 minutes more than the square of the number of data entries.

C. The running time is determined by adding 8 minutes to the number of data entries and squaring the sum.

D. The running time is 8 times as long as the square of the number of data entries.

RSA SecurID®

This RSA device provides a unique code every 60 seconds to prove a user's identity.

The Rise of Quantum Computers

In the coming years, the way data is stored and coded could change. There is a new machine on the horizon. It is called the **quantum computer**.

Quantum computers store data in a new way. While classical computers store data in bit, quantum computers store data in qubits (KYOO-bihts). These qubits store both zeros and ones at the same time.

Chemist Stephen Glasser is famous in the world of quantum computing.

In other words, quantum computers are more flexible about how they store data. This should allow them to process data faster. If these machines live up to the hype, there could be huge benefits. With the help of quantum computing, white hats will be able to locate threats much faster.

Several companies are working to create quantum computers. But building the machines isn't easy. For them to work, they must be in controlled settings. Quantum computers are fragile. Even radio waves can disrupt the machines' ability to store zeros and ones at the same time. This makes the computer unreliable—at least for now. Still, many people are betting on the rise of quantum computers in the near future!

quantum computer core

Shelli's computer is newer and faster than Cat's computer. The friends compare how long it takes for their computers to run some programs.

Rewrite their verbal descriptions as numerical expressions. Use s to represent the number of minutes it takes Shelli's computer to run a program. Use c to represent the number of minutes it takes Cat's computer to run a program.

1. Cat's computer takes "four times as long as Shelli's computer" to run the first program.

2. Shelli's computer takes "ten fewer minutes than Cat's computer" to run the next program.

3. Cat's computer takes "twelve minutes longer than twice the time of Shelli's computer" to run the last program.

4. Together, the friends determine that the average time to run a program is "half the sum of Cat's run time and Shelli's run time."

Dr. Katie Pooley studies a tube that houses a quantum processor.

The Next Generation of Hackers

Today, hacking conferences and **hackathons** are hosted around the world. Some people at the conventions may surprise you. For example, if you attend DEF CON, a giant hacking conference, you might just see members of the U.S. Army joining in the fun.

The world is changing. Governments value hacker training. Having government officials speak at hacking conferences is a big deal. In 2017, the U.S. Army sent Cyber Command officials to DEF CON. The Army was there to teach kids the basics of ethical hacking.

If you have an interest in hacking, the time to start learning is now. At DEF CON, even young kids are welcomed to learn hacking basics! The army also hopes to train a new generation of white hat hackers. Millions of white hats may be needed in coming years. Will you be a part of the next generation of ethical hackers?

Deputy Commanding General for the U.S. Army Cyber Command J. P. McGee speaks about the future of cybersecurity.

Black and white hat hackers race to hack into electronic devices during a DEF CON conference.

LET'S EXPLORE MATH

Imagine that a college started offering students a chance to major in computer science in 2010. The number of computer science students increases each year. College staff use the expression $5 + t^3$ to estimate the number of students, where t represents the number of years since 2010.

1. Estimate the number of students in the computer science program this year.

2. Choose all the expressions you could use to make the same estimate.

   A. $5 + t + t + t$ **C.** $t^3 + 5$ **E.** $5 + t^3$

   B. $5 + t \times t \times t$ **D.** $(5 + t)^3$

Problem Solving

   DEF CON has been held for over 20 years. On average, attendance increases every year. Imagine that the table summarizes approximate attendance at recent DEF CONs. After a worker researches the number of attendees at DEF CON 21, she describes attendance for other DEF CONs as a challenge for her co-worker.

   Put your decoding skills to use. Write numerical expressions for the verbal descriptions, and evaluate them to find the number of attendees. Use *n* to represent the number of attendees. Then, answer the questions to forecast attendance at the next DEF CONs.

1. Based on past attendance information, how many attendees do you expect at DEF CONs 26 and 27? Why?

2. Write verbal descriptions and numerical expressions to match your expected numbers of attendees. Remember to use numbers of attendees from previous DEF CONs in your work.

DEF CON Number	Verbal Description	Numerical Expression	Approximate Number of Attendees
			14,000
21			
22	multiply the number of DEF CON 21 attendees by 3, subtract 12,000, and divide the result by 2		
23	1,000 more than the number of DEF CON 22 attendees		
24	multiply the number of DEF CON 23 attendees by 5, divide the product by 4, and add 500 to the result		
25	4,000 less than double the number of DEF CON 21 attendees		

Glossary

access—a way of being able to use or get something

algorithm—steps used to solve a math or computer problem

alleged—accused of wrongdoing

anonymously—made or done by someone unknown

binary system—a system that represents information using the numbers 0 and 1

cybersecurity—the protection of private digital information

encryption—information that has been changed from one form to another, especially to hide its meaning

esteemed—highly respected

ethical hackers—people who hack legally, often done to test a network's security

hackathons—events where teams of people create new, usable software in just a few days

hacktivists—people who hack information for social or political causes

honed—made better or more effective

malware—software made to infect computers.

mimic—to create the effect of or to look or act like something

quantum computer—a computer that stores information in qubits, units that can hold zeros and ones at the same time

stock photo—a picture that can be bought or sold for commercial purposes

storied—having an interesting history

Index

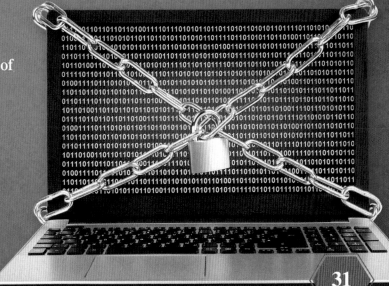

Answer Key

Let's Explore Math

page 7

A, D

page 11

1. 243

2. 59,049

3. No, it is more than double because it was posted at an exponential rate, not multiplied by 2.

4. 1; This is the original post.

page 13

1. **a**. 30 minutes

   b. 50 minutes

   c. 530 minutes; or 8 hours, 50 minutes

   d. 2,030 minutes; or 33 hours, 50 minutes

2. No, Martina only needs to square the number of bugs. She does not need to square the product of 20 and the number of bugs.

page 23

1. B

2. C

3. A

4. D

page 25

1. $4s$, or $4 \times s$

2. $c - 10$

3. $12 + 2s$

4. $(c + s) \div 2$

page 27

1. Answers depend on year. For instance, if it has been 9 years since 2010, the expression is $5 + 9^3$, which has a value of 734 when evaluated.

2. B, C, and E

Problem Solving

DEF CON 22—$(3n - 12,000) \div 2$; 15,000
DEF CON 23—$n + 1,000$; 16,000
DEF CON 24—$500 + \frac{5n}{4}$; 20,500
DEF CON 25—$2n - 4,000$; 24,000

1. Answers should be greater than 24,000 and include reasoning for the estimates. The expected attendees at DEF CON 27 should be greater than the expected attendees at DEF CON 26.

2. Answers should include matching verbal descriptions and numerical expressions that have values of the estimates when evaluated.